# See If I Feel the Same

# See If I Feel the Same

Poems by

Kathaleen Donnelly

© 2025 Kathaleen Donnelly. All rights reserved.
This material may not be reproduced in any form, published,
reprinted, recorded, performed, broadcast,
rewritten, or redistributed without
the explicit permission of Kathaleen Donnelly.
All such actions are strictly prohibited by law.

Cover design by Shay Culligan
Cover image by Kathaleen Donnelly
Photoshopped by Valerie Interligi

ISBN: 978-1-63980-733-8

Kelsay Books
502 South 1040 East, A-119
American Fork, Utah 84003
Kelsaybooks.com

*Dedicated to my
son and daughter-in-law
Keith and Annie*

*&*

*Frances and William, Dorothy and John,
Dorothy M. Weber, Carol, Eileen,
Pat/Bud, Mary and Nancy/Rick*

*&*

*to my beloved Long Island,
home for a lifetime.*

# Acknowledgments

Thank you to the following publications, in which versions of these poems previously appeared:

*Bard's Annual:* "August Days," "Television"
*Brookhaven Arts and Humanities Council:* "A Phenomenal Conversation"
*Long Island Sounds, from Maspeth to Montauk and Beyond:* "IMPOSSIBLE," "Lost in Autumn," "Spring Cleaning," "A Poem for Today"
*Long Islander's Walt's Corner:* "Television"
*Oberon Magazine:* "An Admission," "A Phenomenal Conversation"
*Paumanok, Interwoven:* "Spring Cleaning"
*Paumanok, Poems and Pictures of Long Island:* "Lost in Autumn"
*Paumanok, Transition:* "A Trigger"
*Performance Poets Association Annual Literary Review:* "Whistles," "Solitude," "Some of Us," "Not Spring Yet"
*Princess Ronkonkoma Productions:* "August Days," "A Trigger"
*The Seventh Quarry Poetry Magazine:* "SICU," "Aging Remedy"
*Songs of Seasoned Women:* "Aging Remedy"
*Suffolk County Poetry Review:* "Retreat at Auschwitz, Remembering One Seventy Years Later," "Early Winter Morning"
*Towards Forgiveness:* "Perspectives"
*What Have You Lost and Found:* "The Dig"
*Whispers and Shouts, Anthology of Poetry by Women of Long Island:* "In Belle Terre"
*Writing Outside the Lines:* "Some of Us"

Many thanks to friends
whose voices sing their stories
and who made suggestions
to help me sing mine.

## Pre-Covid
Carmen Bugan
Sasha Ettinger
Adam Fisher
Charles Adés Fishman
Steve Schmidt
Claire Nicolas White
Michelle Whittaker

## Post-Covid
Gladys Henderson
William Heyen
Robert Savino
Carol Schmidt
Barbara Southard
Pramila Venkateswaran
George Wallace

# Contents

In the Sleeping Grass (Winter)

| | |
|---|---|
| Not Spring Yet | 17 |
| Through the Window | 18 |
| Winter Winds | 19 |
| Early Winter Morning | 20 |
| Trees in Wintertime | 21 |
| What I want for Christmas | 22 |
| Robinson's Tea Room | 23 |
| Mid-January | 24 |
| A Winter Walk | 25 |
| March in New York | 26 |

A Tribute to Time (Medicine)

| | |
|---|---|
| Fear | 29 |
| S.I.C.U. | 30 |
| Takotsubo | 31 |
| For Beauty's Sake | 33 |
| New York City | 34 |
| Lost Thing | 37 |
| P.T.S.D. | 38 |
| Inertia | 39 |

What's Next? (Spring) 41

| | |
|---|---|
| A Poem for Today | 43 |
| Spring Cleaning | 44 |
| Aging Remedy | 45 |
| The Ocean Side of the Island | 47 |
| Misty Night | 48 |
| Sometimes | 49 |

It's All Wrong (War)

| | |
|---|---:|
| 'When It Rains It Pours' | 53 |
| On a Farm in Poland, 1939 | 54 |
| Conscientious Objector, 1942 | 55 |
| Beyond the Edges | 56 |
| Retreat at Auschwitz | 59 |
| War in Iraq and Afghanistan, 2006 | 62 |
| Peace and War | 63 |
| Darfur, Sudan | 64 |
| War in Syria | 65 |
| Television | 66 |

My Mind Follows (Summer)

| | |
|---|---:|
| A Phenomenal Conversation | 69 |
| Evening on the Beach | 70 |
| The Dig | 71 |
| One Strand Too Many | 72 |
| Some of Us | 73 |
| Swimming with the Jelly Fish | 74 |
| August Days | 75 |
| Summer's End | 76 |

I Would Like to Have Known You (Relationships)

| | |
|---|---:|
| A Trigger | 79 |
| Perspectives | 80 |
| IMPOSSIBLE | 81 |
| Skimming | 82 |
| Dear Grandmother, | 83 |

See If I Feel the Same (Fall)

| | |
|---|---|
| An Admission | 87 |
| Solitude | 88 |
| Whistles | 89 |
| Lost in Autumn | 90 |
| Grandmother | 91 |
| In Belle Terre | 92 |
| Almost November | 93 |
| Candlelight | 94 |

In
the
Sleeping
Grass

(Winter)

# Not Spring Yet

The disc stopped playing on the CD player.
I reach to lift a needle, flip it to its other side.

I think of my grandparents walking
hand-in-hand to occasional concerts

live in the park or a silent film at the cinema—
piano player in the corner.

When they could listen to music
through an AM radio, did the high tech

make them reminisce?

Winter is coming. I push a button
for Brahms 3$^{rd}$ movement to begin.

I'd like it to play all the way till spring,

or have spring begin
when the disc turns itself off—

skip

like my old vinyls.

# Through the Window

Glass thick with frost,
bedroom windows obscure
frenzied snowflakes in white sky.

In early hours of morning I linger awhile,
imagine the land deep in snow.
It suits my mood, locked in to my home,

my bed, under blankets, soft pillow,
warm glow from a tungsten light-bulb.
The world can do without me for a day.

I want to spend it with my inner self,
see what's at the bottom of things—
solid ground beneath soft-white cover.

# Winter Winds

Winter is for slow-moving mornings,
wondering how the sun looks
above thick white clouds.

Warm woolens to the breakfast table,
hands cup hot porcelain. We sip Tetley tea
watching wild winds blow.

On thin layers of glass, crystal flakes
warm breath cannot melt, take up more
and more of the square frame between us.

Sheltered, we give permission to winter's wrath—
it is an understanding.
Ha! As if we had a say in it.

# Early Winter Morning

Walking up a steep hill between bare trees
to see the sunrise, I stop when I reach the top,

catch my breath, close my eyes, feel warmth
on bare skin, face reddened in cold air.

A rising orange star turns yellow,
lights on for the day.

The new day's dawn, it cannot be stopped.
I greet it with a long drawn-out sigh,

lungs empty old air, fill with new.
Steps, one after the other, down, down the dune

till I reach the ocean's shore. The smell
of brine permeates, I feel salt water stir within.

Small curls at water's edge unravel
just as they always do.

A sandpiper scuttles past me,
kin in tow.

# Trees in Wintertime

On this December night all is still,
no wind rushes through frozen shadows.
Snow-covered branches sigh quietly
till warm sun comes to their rescue.
They'll wait.

Brown leaves dead and gone,
buried deep underfoot,
severed from all ties,
protect their mother's roots—
purpose in their demise.

This is a night for reflection. A walk
through these woods a solitary tryst,
no one ventures out to meet you.
Stand still, try to be one of them . . .
until you breathe, give yourself away.

# What I want for Christmas

    is that way of thinking
that allows a person
to just push forward,
no worry or concern
about what others think,
pave a straight path
neither bending or yielding
to calls or commands
like the leader-of-the-crowd
whose focus becomes
that of his followers . . .

or a candlestick with scented
candle, the non-toxic kind.
That would be nice.

# Robinson's Tea Room

In the corner she sat, small table for two,
blue cotton cushion on a wooden chair settled
her in, same as yesterday and the day before.
One expected her here, she was always here.

Lavender and white pinstripes on wallpaper
seemed to extend to her man-tailored shirt;
white wooden wainscoting matched her cardigan,
I couldn't help but notice.

She sipped English tea, two sugars, dash of cream,
hands wrapped around her china-cup
warming them, a place to rest
as snowflakes fell softly to the sidewalk.

Clientele came and left on this gray December day,
cold draft each time the door swung open,
bells ringing. One tea bag kept her cup drinkable,
she didn't seem to notice.

She nibbled on a scone with raspberry jam
or a biscuit with clotted cream and every
hour or so, she'd glance through the glass
as if waiting for an overdue friend.

No one appeared, harried, apologetic.
She'd glance at her watch,
reach for her coat, lower her eyes,
leave deep in thought.

# Mid-January

Walking out into an open field
        once overrun with wild grasses and brush

now a fine silk sheet
        under distant stars, quarter moon.

Warm breath travels through cold air,
        a visible exchange.

Distant echoes,
        frozen branches snap into twigs.

My footsteps interrupt a silent song,
        sink into crushed softness,

mar this immaculate scene
        fallen to earth this night.

I want to blend into glittering whiteness—
        not take anything away.

# A Winter Walk

February begins with a bright warm sun,
clean dry air. I step out into winter,
bare skin spared from blast of cold sting.

Without snow and ice covering roadways
and lawns, I look for snowdrops to appear,
pay attention this time round.

A right-hand turn at the corner
would lead me down Cordwood Path
to the Sound. I'd walk in the shade.

So I'll turn left toward Fifty Acres Road,
let the sun follow me
like a spellbound lover.

# March in New York

The days grow longer now, I breathe easy
knowing the dark days of deep snow

are exhausted in January, diminished in February,
nearly gone altogether in March.

But only nearly. My red cast-iron pot filled to the brim
with hot peppermint tea boils over on the stovetop

reminding me never to expect anything
to be easy, predictable, compliant.

Tomorrow I'll expect a December-like storm,
blustering winds, finger-numbing cold,

rejoice if I can find pink and purple crocuses
in the sleeping grass.

A
Tribute
to
Time

(Medicine)

# Fear

I leave the *Tiger Lily Cafe,*
East Main Street, Port Jefferson Village,
hummus, smoothie—*Purple Rain,*
organic Columbian coffee w/ soy,
read poetry by David Whyte
to new-age music
on a soft cushioned couch,

then drive down Nicholls Road to a friend.

I pull up to the second intersection
suddenly overcome with fear
that Stony Brook University Hospital,
my employer over thirty years,
will spot me passing by,
send out giant forceps, extract me from my car,
furnish me with a pair of scrubs,
cry mercy for understaffing.

It is my day off,
*goddamnit!*

# S.I.C.U.

*(Surgical Intensive Care Unit)*


A small room overlooks the parking lot
with a dozen colored lights—
alarms, settings, waveforms.
An injured boy's life is in jeopardy.

Intubation tube sits in his airway,
ventilator breathes a set tidal volume
every six seconds, oxygen, peep, P.I.P., flow.
A Swan-Ganz enters through an introducer

to his subclavian vein, another catheter
in his radial artery, his penis draining urine.
A bolt measures pressure
a swollen brain makes against a hard skull.

Tube-fed through his nostril into his duodenum,
eyes taped closed,
passive range of motion,
soft music he may or may not hear.

The air mattress tilts left, then right
while a beating heart forms an electrical pattern
above an a-line wave on a monitor screen.
Paralyzed with Pavulon, sedated with morphine—

he will never be the same as yesterday,
on his skate board, soaring downhill at top speed.

# Takotsubo

Soft blond curls strewn across the pillow
catch my eye as I walk through the CCU,
Cardiac Care Unit, and wonder
*why is she here?*, young for this department.

Fifty-two-year-old female,
Past Medical History: none
Past Surgical History: none
No known drug allergies.
Family history: non-contributory
Social History: No smoking, drugs, alcohol abuse.
Married with two teenage children,
stay at home mom, member of the PTA,
runner of 5K marathons.

Pt was admitted to the Emergency Department,
Code H, chest pain with ST elevations on EKG,
QT prolongation, elevated cardiac enzymes—
markers for a heart attack.
Sent stat to the cardiac cath lab.

Much to everyone's surprise, her coronaries
are 'clean', no disease, but her left ventricle
is dilated, apical akinesis.

Catecholamines had surged
through her arteries, an adrenalin rush
that left her weak, stunned her muscle—
ejection fraction so low she requires
an intra-aortic balloon pump for support.

Without pressors to support blood pressure,
careful monitoring of her vital signs,
this mother of two teens would be gone,

all because of a late night phone call
from an old friend . . . and bad news.

The ballooning of this chamber
reminds doctors in Japan
of an ancient urn to catch octopi.
An octopus pot.
Americans learn the term, call it
Broken Heart Syndrome.

If our minds have the power to undo us,
might a different message cure?

# For Beauty's Sake

A human being, female form, lies on her reclined
beach chair, blue crisscrossed with yellow, red.
It has been three hours now, I know, I've been here four.

It's 90 degrees, sky bright, not a whisper of cloud.
Sun's hot rays strike golden-pebbled sand relentlessly,
I wear sandals, spare bare feet.

She does not move, probably asleep. I notice
her same position as I trek back and forth on this
north shore beach, concession stand, water's edge.

In between chapters I take a plunge into wet blue,
submerge in cool relief, swim under baking sun,
return to my umbrella and book, renewed.

I worry for her skin, so much exposure,
sun poisoning, first-degree burns, maybe second;
she's slowly being cooked.

I am a mother, sister, daughter, nurse, want to tell her
to "cover up," "take care." It's not my business, I know—
where do I draw my own line?

She has black hair, that's good, not fair:
Ireland, Iceland, Scotland, Wales. Perhaps she has on
lots of lotion or an abundance of melanin, olive skin.

My quiet day under sun and sky
is disrupted by unsolicited concern.
I don't want to see her at work.

# New York City

I meet Theresa, fellow Nurse Practitioner
at the LIRR in St. James, sleepy town, Long Island,
who will commute back and forth daily,
arrive at the conference, 9am, 3 days of lectures,
Pri-Med, Jacob Javits Center, 11th Ave. and 34th Street,
sweaters and sweat socks in the AC,
T-shirts in the 80-degree outside world,

and think of Paul Winter, his Summer Solstice Consort
at precisely the dawn of day, 4:30 AM,
Cathedral of St. John the Divine, Amsterdam and 112th,
celebrate life, light through stained glass
on the last day of the conference,
and I want to go, but can't decide,
do I pull an all-nighter?, I'm in my 50s, not my teens,
and I want to know what Paul is thinking

as I walk towards The Leo House, a guesthouse—
old refuge for German immigrants,
23rd Street between 8th and 9th, clean, quiet,
no bed bugs, great rate per night,

have my palm read next door by Patricia,
Romanian, she gets it all right, but has two
risk factors, smoking, high BMI, and I wonder
if she is post-menopausal, want to say something
but don't, she's psychic, she should know,

meet an old friend for dinner who thinks he married
the wrong woman, remembers only the good times,
who is willing to walk with me to St. Vincent's Hospital,

my School of Nursing, 12th Street between 6th and 7th
Avenue, now all boarded up and a part of me
feels a great loss, like an old friend gone forever,

have mushrooms and artichoke, third evening in a row,
with black olives I've asked the gourmet chef to add at
EOLO, SICILIA A TRAVOLA, 7th Ave. between 21st and 22nd,
wonder if I've offended her or has she changed the menu,

have a Quantum Biofeedback session with Julia,
Hungarian, who promises me I've had my stressors
corrected energetically, which I need
for the last day of lectures—

Pradaxa can't be reversed, one's FEV1/FVC ratio
should be over 70%, constrictive vs. obstructive,
most lung nodules are benign, there are false negative
BNPs and normal ejection fractions in diastolic heart failure,

and my friend Donna wants to talk about everything
as we walk towards EOLO to have my favorite dish
after her work at the Visiting Nursing Service
on 34th Street between 5th and 6th,

wonder if Patricia has COPD while I wait for Donna
to have her world explored through her palm,
then see *The Tree of Life* with Sean Penn, who smokes,
at the theater on 23rd Street between 7th and 8th,

same street as The Leo House I learn has an 8$^{th}$ floor
full of nuns which explains the crucifix over my bed
in my 'hotel' room, chapel on the 2$^{nd}$ floor, reminds
me of my dormitory at St. Vincent's,

and Donna and I talk about the film, our work
and our issues till 1am, set the clock for 3am, wake
to the alarm to decide if we will head up
to the Cathedral of St. John the Divine
as if there was a decision,
go back to sleep and wonder

what is Paul thinking?

# Lost Thing

It was once in my hand,
I owned it, held it, used it.
I know this is true,
I swear to God.

I have forgotten
to remember where I left it
only discovering now that
it is missing from its original place.

I don't remember putting it
where it is, leaving it behind.
It so completely escaped me
to take that extra step.

As I search,
retrace those steps I can recall,
I find myself in the searching
a new person, aged, forgetting things.

I need for it to have a conscience,
miss me as much as I miss it,
find me, after all,
I am easily found.

# P.T.S.D.

Memories
always present, buried deep inside—
slowly siphoned from that space
that belongs to yesterday, over, done,

return as they once were, alive, vivid,
rain daily into your day,
drench covers you sleep under,
carpet you tread through to the tea kettle,

pour into your drink, into your body
like a fountain ever puddling its details—
into your core, the ones you cannot forget,
cannot let go of,

the ones that make you wait at the door,
wait for rain to surrender once again,
fully and whole, into the wet, into the day
as if they had come calling.

# Inertia

Sitting on my brown velour sofa,
my mind is on hold.
The day begins the moment I decide.
I don't.

Seconds turn into hours, I own them, they are mine.
No expenditure of energy, no need to sleep,
suspended in time, aware nothing need occur
right now, or all day.

The phone needn't be answered, mail read.
I could fast for a day, there's enough reserve.
I claim this day a holiday from all things
in the outside world,

the other,
        total cognizance,
              of time,
                      for time's sake . . .

```
                        begin
                          e
                l        forever
                a        o    n
                t        r    days
A tribute to time.
w          r    h
hours           e    s
i               never
l          w    c
eons       h    o
   o       e    now
   o       n    d
   n       decades
           v
           e
       ever
         e
       vegetate
```

What's
Next?

(Spring)

# A Poem for Today

To wake at 7am, clock ticking, is a gift.
Body, still alive, drifts back into pleasure
of rest, conscious without dreams.

Bed surrounded with books, journals,
newspaper clippings, memos; words sink in
through synapses at their own pace.

How many neurons do I have
before information has nowhere to go?
Then all I will have left is what I have known.

That would not be good.
I embrace this lazy morning of which
there are too few. Let the day take me.

On my kitchen countertop: electric tea pot,
filtered water for organic coffee, coconut milk,
Trader Joe's pumpkin pancakes, virgin olive oil

rather than melted butter, two eggs instead of three.
I should live a long healthy life. It is the maple syrup
that fills me with regret—maybe not so long.

Today will be different from all the others.
I say this at 7am.

# Spring Cleaning

When you said you were coming to visit,
I noticed cobwebs in all the corners
so took down every domicile
of my quiet eight-legged tenants.

Because you said you were coming,
I found the clothesline to hang linens,
laundered towels, fluffed pillows, vacuumed,
washed dishes contented where they were left.

So excited was I that you were coming, I put
the books back on the bookshelf, piled papers,
dusted lampshades, and with a soft cotton cloth
wiped family photos you'd wish to see.

When you called and said you were not coming,
I was not sorry to have done a 'spring cleaning'.
Perhaps you should tell me to expect you
around this time each year.

# Aging Remedy

I've decided
to start counting backward,
this birthday I'll turn 52, again.

54 will be 51.
At 55 I'll celebrate my $50^{th}$
with my 'kid' sister, secretly
take myself out on the town.

65, the new 40.
Climb the Tetons, visit art galleries
in Jackson Hole. Have a film
festival in my living room. BYOB.

75, 30.
Yoga, Pilates, exotic trips
just because. Study a second
language, learn to play the cello.

At 85, 20.
I'll buy a tie-dye dress, braid my hair
with flowers, paint a peace sign
on my forehead, blast Jethro Tull,
dance barefoot around the backyard
in a mid-April spring rain.

At 95, 10.
Green plaid uniform, penny-loafers,
ice skating, sledding, Irish tap—
Beatles on the Ed Sullivan Show. Ask for
a sticker for every library book read.

If I make it to 100,
reruns of the Little Rascals, Bowery Boys,
Charlie Chan and his Number One Son,
watch Abbott and Costello meet Frankenstein
on a black and white T.V., find a small
tree to climb, children to play with.

# The Ocean Side of the Island

*Jones Beach with Maxwell Corydon Wheat, Jr.*


I walked a south shore beach this cold gray day,
stepped around channeled whelk,
colorful cockle shells, chitons clinging to rocks.
Dragged boots in wet sand
littered with carcasses from the deep sea.
Spider crabs, oysters, mussels, half buried
horseshoe crab—remnant of a high tide.

Gypsy moth caterpillars convened in pine tents,
beach plum berries lit up morning mist.
Japanese pines dropped cones sprouting fresh ones.
Millet graced sandy turf.

Seagulls dove from great heights for their supper,
disappeared into blue—found its treasure.
Red knots and oystercatchers combed the beach,
graced it with their presence.
Least terns and osprey, eagles and hawks,
all came and went on this bay by the sea.

Is this nature then, one life surviving
at the expense of another? All predators, all prey—
natural underlings born to be a meal?

I think of the horseshoe crab stuck in sand.
Seaweed and salt water had no premeditation.

# Misty Night

Into haze, dark, foreboding, a sky
too high to touch, I settle for mist
sent down to coat the earth.

Enveloped in mystery, one bright
and distant cloud passes between earth
and moon, gives life to shape and form.

By morning it will be gone
or have stayed in place while
earth revolved.

I'll miss the moist air that overtook the sky
where I could lose myself—
surrender to the night.

# Sometimes

   the feel of a ripe plum on your lips,
taste on your tongue, have you forget
you are creeping along at 5 MPH in your car
on the Southern State Parkway
somewhere between Merrick and Massapequa.

Sometimes the sound of bowed strings
on a cello, flute slipping in between fifths,
viola soft and low, make you forget
you are waiting on line at the deli section,
Wild Pacific Salmon on sale, *Wild by Nature.*

Sometimes the smell of pine along the edge
of the Nissequogue as your canoe drifts downstream,
taste of ginger beer as you paddle gently with the current,
make you forget the untended garden, unpaid bills,
the 9 to 5 waiting for you on Monday morning.

Sometimes, vast blueness, clouds shape-shifting,
our yellow star high in the sky, bound barefoot by
gravity to a circling orb, makes you forget yourself,
who you are, what you are — quiets the concerns
about *what's next.*

It's
All
Wrong

(War)

## 'When It Rains It Pours'

When it rains
he looks to find the details,
the reason every raindrop falls,

its angle, slant,
way of being
in relation to it all;

dropping in tandem, in disarray,
ambivalent, unsure
of falling at all.

Unanswered questions,
in the rain
falling,

he stands very still
drowning
in nothing he caused.

# On a Farm in Poland, 1939

Horses graze in an open meadow, cows
milked for the breakfast table, still warm,
borscht, groats, potatoes, wholemeal rye.

Sarah and Simon spend summer days
climbing trees, chasing butterflies,
collecting dandelion for mama's tea,
tata's wine, fireflies in evening light.

Horsetails swat flies away, sun shines,
clouds drift, children play without a care.
No one taught them suspicion, caution,

fear of strangers, when to hide. When
two men in uniform drive down the dirt road
alongside their family farm and wave to them,
beckon them to come, they do.

Lifted to the back of a truck, friends recognized
from their talmudic school, a comfort. Talking,
laughing till brought to a camp, fate unknown.

Butterflies flit in hot summer air,
dandelions light up an open field,
horses whinny, rest their muzzles
on each other's backs while

mama sets a table, milk and bread,
calls out for them to come in from play
before sending them to their room for a nap.

# Conscientious Objector, 1942

Northern Lights undulate across a night sky,
green and gold. When they were gone
he was left with moon and starlight. Stephan
watched his exhaled breath in cold dark air.

How much easier, he thought, if it were just him.
A war raging, not possible to bring enough
provisions to this remote place in the forest,
protect his wife and child.

What were his choices?
To be part of the madness, the war machine,
'a good soldier?' In the end he could see
he would be glad he fled, he was sure of it.

Hunting, gathering, it had been done before.
Rising with the sun, sleeping when it set,
he listened to the silent night,
prayed it stayed that way.

# Beyond the Edges

*in Ukraine*


He traveled alone, no signs to follow.
Sunflowers everywhere randomly
in fields along train tracks, no one
watching over them.

In his youth, his family kept their small
village thriving. He knew this, he had helped.
They were the quiet folk behind the scenes,
made everything work—

collected wood cut for fires, gathered seeds,
sowed, weeded, watered, harvested. Land of plenty.
He helped dig graves, said prayers, buried their dead,
watched new generations take their place.

He could hear sounds in his mind—
town folk talking, horses neighing,
birds flying in flocks, swooping down,
disappearing in brush for supper, sleep.

A few small structures remained,
he looked for something familiar, sure
he was in the right spot. Now—
open fields, long dirt roads, setting sun.

*Wall of victims.*

*A woman who had a name.*

# Retreat at Auschwitz
## Remembering One, Eighty Years Later

Pebbles shuffle underfoot
with winter boots, the same that flew
through heavy air when NAZI boots
marched through here, Poland's land.

Under pale blue sky that reached all the way
to Hawaii where people ran barefoot on soft sand,
dove into ocean waves, held breath to swim deep
with underwater creatures, caught them for dinner,

at the same time, under same blue sky
brushed with whispers of white,
birds flew nest to nest, quiet source of serenity—
smoke billowed, floated towards heaven.

Oak trees sway in Autumn wind,
shed yellow leaves, falling . . . falling,
resting on blades of green grass.
Did they do the same then?

The warmth of a November sun rests
on my face, heat in crisp cool air.
Did *she* feel it too, while she, her family,
her friends waited in a line? Waited.

The evening before, she washed her hair,
curled it with rags, beer, slept on a bumpy head.
In the morning, put on her lipstick carefully,
washed dishes, ironed her dress, his shirt,

swept the floor, closed all the shutters, turned
down the heat. Children's outfits selected,
best for travel. She packed suitcases, not too heavy,
looked into her husband's eyes. No answers.

Teeth brushed, hair brushed, ready for a trip,
an adventure, the unknown, sleepy children kept close.
They boarded a train, endless hours till the door
finally opened, hand extended to help her dismount.

Then husband one way, children another.
Women just following orders took everything,
her suitcase, earrings, necklace, wedding ring,
watch, looked into her mouth for gold.

How could anyone for no reason at all, take her money,
identification, photographs? Tell her to take off her coat
and scarf, skirt and blouse, shoes and stockings,
undergarments—leave her naked, shave off all her hair?

So much taking.

Did she have the same shade of skin, same color
eyes? Did she speak the same language, have friends
in common? Did she go to the same school,
have the same teachers, study side by side?

Did she go to the same cinema on Saturday nights,
laugh at Charlie Chaplin, Tran und Helle, listen
to the same music, Mozart, Strauss? Were they going
to be related by marriage, share a family circle?

Had she gone to her church, synagogue
in days before, prayed for peace,
asked for a safer world?
Did she feel she knew her God?

Looking at layers of barbed wire, electrified,
tall towers, stone-faced men, women, angry
dogs, loaded guns, weak with hunger, thirst,
what were her choices?

I imagine she dreamed of escape, adrenaline
pumping, only to arrive on the other side
of the fence where a bald head, striped pajamas,
the way she carried herself, *the way she walked,*

would give her away. All hope dwindled until gone.

Workers, *obeying orders,*
new laws from authorities—
leading her to a shower
knowing it would be her last.

Yellow leaves fall now as they did then.
Pale blue sky goes on forever and ever.
Green grass grows all summer alongside
these ruins.

Germany's love for the Fatherland,
a national scar, forever and ever,
and the memory of what happened here,
to her.

# War in Iraq and Afghanistan, 2006

The news talks of war:
'We should stay the course',
'We should retreat'.

58,000 dead in Viet Nam,
my class mates, our brothers, future husbands.

Now, we are outraged by 2000;
our daughters, our sons.

Progress?

While politicians argue,
the flesh on my son's bones
is in jeopardy.

# Peace and War

I curl up on my couch, pillows in position,
wrapped in a quilt after hours of work.
That world done for the day, my eyes gravitate to the window,
green grass, green bushes, green trees. An essay on green.
Leaves rattle against glass as warm winds sift through the screen.
Peace.

It's 7 p.m., PBS: Jim Lehrer, Judy Woodruff, Gwen Ifill,
a scene from across the planet, an explosion. A young man
has taken his own life, many with him. Two hundred men
no longer live their lives. Bloody body parts strewn about—
men shout, women wail, children scream. An essay on red.
Jim cuts to a different glimpse of the world.
Enough.

But I know it's not over, not for them, not for a lifetime.
Wives without husbands, children without fathers,
sisters without brothers, missing persons at the workplace.

What would I do without my legs? My arms?
My face disfigured? My mind lost? Loved ones gone?
Maybe one of these things?
No.

Winter has left behind old brown leaves.
They rattle against glass as warm winds sift
through the screen on this peaceful spring evening.
Here.

# Darfur, Sudan

Hot sun envelops desert floor, her small village in Africa.
Straw huts break stifling heat beaming down relentlessly,
her home for a lifetime. Sandy paths between families,
neighbors known since birth, she begins this day like any other.

Girlfriends meet at the water spigot, they like the same boy.
She is dressed to impress, orange and red. Shy glances,
he responds with indifference, too young, joins the men.

Her father works in the fields, she has never known hunger.
Sound of a drumbeat intermingles with clay pots clacking,
mother prepares her meal.

Bushy hillsides in the distance seem to have no end;
each blade of grass perfectly still in the windless air
she dances in. It is a day like any other . . .

till Janjaweed mounted on horseback, a mission—
    straw burns,
        bullets penetrate,
            blood flows,
                voices silenced.

Her life-force erased in seconds,
no one left to call her name,
say she ever was.

# War in Syria

It is only distance that keeps sounds of bombs
from my living-room window.

I cannot see your house crumble
from my front porch

or hear the growling of your child's belly as I slice open
an English Muffin and try to decide, *butter or jam?*

I do not see your brother's gaping wound
as I place a Band-Aid over my paper-cut

or need to duck bullets missing their targets
killing your cousin on his wedding day, 'collateral damage.'

I want to stretch my arms into the TV,
grab you by your shirt collar, family holding tight,

put you all in my guest room
till the war is over.

# Television

The same mass-media
that links me to the fine arts,
ballets, symphonies, Broadway plays
in New York City—in my living room,
a Ceili in Ireland, cycling—Tour de France,
horse racing, car racing, hearts racing,
Olympics on the other side of the globe,
antiques worth fortunes in attics, storage closets,
renditions of old novels I'll never have time to read,

makes me feel guilty, to have so much,
when the same source of information,
in color, surround sound, floods my living room
with the cries of children who live with so little,

no television, to see
it's all wrong.

My
Mind
Follows


(Summer)

# A Phenomenal Conversation

We talked of clouds
suspended, floating
whispers of cirrus
inference of cumulus
chance of rain

Our steps in tandem
we talked of forgettable things
dragged toes in wet sand, semi-circle
patterns, while miniature curls unraveled
quiet roar along the shoreline

We talked of nothing important
while rays of white sunlight
pierced through clouds
illuminated blue-green—
connected us to heaven

Seagulls studied low tide
hovered over their supper
while we talked of small matters
walked towards an orange star
as it set where sea and sky meet

quietly bowed
        said good-night
                and disappeared

even though we were still talking

# Evening on the Beach

A small brown skinned boy stands at the shoreline
hurling flat rocks into the Sound,
surprised each time they don't skim the surface,
tries again, and again.

Seagulls glide along water's crest
towards me as I float atop, not edible, fly on.
Near the shore they avoid airborne rocks,
sense danger. How do their bird brains know?

Exposed green-haired boulders announce
low tide. I swim three feet above a sandy floor.

The sun peeks between clouds.
Sun rays strike the sea, leave a shimmering trail.
I could follow it, circumvent the globe
if land mass didn't block the way.

My young friend leaves me,
I am alone on a beach on the north shore
of Long Island. Where is everyone
on a hot mid-August eve?

No matter.
I am with the shimmering sea.

# The Dig

Blydenburgh Park, mid-summer day,
calls me to its water's edge, soft light breeze,
tall pines shading moss-covered stones.

I wander through green-canopied paths
drawn towards movement of water—
belly full of life, swimming, breathing.

Mother Earth after centuries of seasons,
curious tear in her edging, I dig deeper—
a disintegrating satchel,

arrowheads no owner to claim.
I examine this find, instant connection
to another being and time.

# One Strand Too Many

I respect the work of this spider,
appreciate the time and effort
she took to construct her web, her crib,
finding the right spot, squatter's rights,
then round and round, symmetric, even,
done by the time I return from an errand.
I wonder if webs are all alike or is each one
an individual signature? I would leave it be,
respect her space except for that one long
viscid filament, anchor across my path.

## Some of Us

Some of us belong to a time,
it was then we came alive,
tasted fresh air, ran free in summer heat,
breathed energy, exhaled fire.

When that time slipped away
we remained in its grasp
unable to rise with the tide,
change direction with moon's pull.

I belong to a time and place.
With braided hair, tie-dyed skirt,
sandals and Grateful Dead riffs,
walk this island's wooded hills,

bicycle its winding paths,
up, down and around
till I reach its rocky shore.
I submerge into salty sea,

heart beating to its rhythm,
swim towards its perimeter,
bury feet in hot sand, narrow
strip beneath the dunes.

The sky changes, blue with blazing sun
to stormy gloom and back,
but I do not change with it as I age
as long as I am here.

# Swimming with the Jelly Fish

Hands in prayer
I slip into blue sea,
slice through its surface,
feel a cold thrill
in hot, humid air.

My body afloat,
I propel deeper in,
emerge only for breath,
acquiesce to water's pull,
change of mood.

Sudden sting,
a thousand pins pricking,
hairy tentacles claim
the shoreline. Skin on fire,
subtle, but unforgiving.

Nowhere to escape,
small translucent creatures
fold and unfold all around.
I am more afraid of them
then they of me

so return
to bake in hot sun,
remedy to pain,
and wait, edgily,
for their season to pass.

# August Days

Days grow shorter now. It's only August,
too soon to be reminded of winter's darkness.

Old wooden fences in Nissequogue
left behind a century or two,
   when dirt roads had hand-painted signs
   and one depended on neighbors,
bend and bow,
keep nothing on either side.

Sparrows in large flocks covet a grassy field,
a pony flicks its black tail at Waterford Stables
   on Branglebrink Road.
They don't mind each other,
soft wind makes all things quiet.

Weeping Willows drape long hair
over small pines that hover
   above a sassafras hedge.
The sun dims its light
   so much earlier in the evenings—
shades of green turn to gray.

All of this will still be here
in brighter hours of the days,
   even when I am not.
Makes me want to carve
my name into something.

# Summer's End

Winds pick up from the north,
soft whispers in blue sky,
gentler in early evening light.
September is still summer, not here
to remind us of the end of anything.

Still time for bare feet and beach sand
before seagulls and geese migrate.
Collecting feathers, seashells, pebbles
with the same color in jars of salt water—
bringing the ocean home.

Swimsuits, sweatshirts, flip-flops,
rocking the night away lying criss-cross
on a hammock stretched between two red maples.
Watching the sun at day's end
set between crimson clinging to boughs.

My body melts into the present.
My mind follows.

I
Would
Like
to
Have
Known
You

(Relationships)

# A Trigger

*(for Keith)*

I open the dictionary,
English, derived from the Germanic,
my language, old as the 5$^{th}$ century,
Webster, unabridged,
spots of mold on its pages,
five inches thick, used as a foot stool,
uniting people under one tongue

and notice the date of publication,
1977, the year my son was born.
There is before him
and then, him.
All of my heart, all of my life
wrapped up in a bundle of knitted stitches
in a world all his own, in my world altogether.

I dreamed of a life I could not give him,
made plans beyond reach.
I can only hope he knows
somewhere within, buried in his solar plexus,
that from the moment he was conceived,
a spark deep inside my womb
growing into his life—

that he never belonged to me,
I belonged to him.

# Perspectives

A leap, that's what it takes,
settled ground,
a certain sense of assuredness,

not that water won't run hot
or the ceiling won't collapse
under the weight of the universe,

rain drops won't find their way
to your forehead while you sleep
or furniture won't hold the carpet down,

but that your inner world
is a safe place to be.
What runs through your mind

is worthy of embrace,
your utmost consideration,
and maybe, for a while,

the revolving of your world.
This is what allows me to know you,
who you really are.

# IMPOSSIBLE

I put a soft cushioned chair
in the hall for you to sit.
You chose the stoop
and left the hall empty.

I cooked a potato-leek soup
on the stove for you to eat.
You decided
this was a good day to fast.

I opened the heavy wooden door
to the house for you to walk through.
That moment, apparently,
was a good time to stroll.

I asked you to be here when I got home
to keep you safe and sound.
You left for a private place
and now I cannot find you.

# Skimming

Sweet nothings,
empty embrace,
words that glide over
still shallow waters.
No waves today.

Invitation without warning
not to engage
while sipping hot herbal tea,
rejoicing over colorful salads.
No spice today.

Visiting old memories selected
with care, ones that make
us smile. Wondering what's
wrong with everybody else.
No truth today.

# Dear Grandmother,

We never met.
Who were you? Does your soul
hover above or around—who are you?

I talk of your 17-year-old experience
in a sentence, 'Pregnant in 1930'.
The words slip from my tongue

as if it were less than a tragedy
that must have colored your entire being
all the days that you breathed—

every waking moment, every minute of sleep.
When did you notice your body changing
from a girl's to a mother's?

Was the child growing in your belly
by consent . . . or not?
Did you know this boy or man,

father to my mother? How did you feel
about being sent away? How did it go
when you returned?

Did our Catholic Church consider you
wayward or naive? How did it feel
to give your child away?

Did you watch her grow from a distance
or try to forget? Did you learn her name,
did you name her? Did you hold her, feed her,

love her for awhile, want to keep her,
raise her on your own? Did this secret
quiver inside of you, yearning to be set free?

Why did you not marry, 17 years old in 1930?
Too bad you could not see into the future,
see how forgiving your child and grandchildren

would be, how the morays of the times would
change about being unmarried and pregnant at 17.
I would like to have known you.

See
If
I
Feel
the
Same

(Fall)

# An Admission

I admit I heard you tell me
everything you wanted to say

but wind rustling in a great white oak
where a robin fought the draft
made rust-colored leaves rain
across an open grassy meadow
pointing the way all things
not stationary would blow,

all the while you told me
what you wanted me to hear.

I imagined being one of those leaves
or a robin redbreast's feather
loosened in the inrush of current,
floating without care or concern

while you talked in past tenses,
what I should have known.

I wondered if I might land softly
like my updraft robin in his nest,
in our home, be stationary
with you

and talk in present tense.

# Solitude

I caught myself just in time
enjoying solitude.

Looking out the window—
leaves cannot waltz on windless autumn days,
they fall silently, collage earth's floor.

Crickets set the beat
for green to turn orange and red.
There is geometry in naked branches.

The warm sun flirts, entices,
I succumb.

In my pajamas while the neighborhood sleeps,
I walk down a quiet side road,

listen thru headphones to Mozart,
interpret landscapes for Van Gogh's brush,
read Whitman when I reach the shoreline.

Solitude undone.
I am alive, now more than ever,
spending my day with the dead.

# Whistles

In my neighborhood roads and lanes,
canopy of thick forested green,
hints of life down suburban driveways, an inlet
where pavement turns to gravel, grass, sand, sea,

I found an acorn top stranded,
a memory rekindled, making the sound
of a whistle when two pursed lips failed.
With two thumb joints kissing,

a deep breath exhaled
as if playing a fine instrument, a shrill so piercing
it was surely heard by every dog's ear
before bouncing off a passing satellite

to dolphins off the Californian coast,
harmonized with an opera in China,
distracted children in Siberian classrooms,
blended with didgeridoos of Aboriginal Australians.

Once more, acorn top in proper position
full breath . . .
I hear only the sound of air.
It takes practice to be a child.

# Lost in Autumn

Dry leaves
crackle underfoot
in a forest of
fallen songs.

Gray clouds
hover overhead
in a sky of
remembered dreams.

Morning rain
brightens tired browns
in a puddle of
spoken words.

Misty drizzle
lingers mid-air
in a sea of
thoughts undone.

# Grandmother

In a small room
on the second floor
with an open window
the door is closing.

In an armchair,
a lit corner
with a book open,
she glances upward.

Autumn breeze
turns old pages
abruptly,
she doesn't notice.

The book drops,
door slams,
she closes her eyes,
absorbs the sun.

## In Belle Terre

She put down her black ink pen, pushed away
from her desk, stood up from her soft cushioned
chair that had come to fit, reached up for her
coat and scarf draped over an open door,
buttoned-up to brace crisp air, unable to think
of anything but you.

Down a dirt path through woods,
bare oak boughs, her steps shuffled
damp yellow leaves, crunched acorn tops
robbed of their seed she did not bother
to step around—only thoughts of you.

Reaching the cliff's edge overlooking the Sound,
she walked with one foot threatening to tip her
down the sand dune to the sea.
Waves crashed and withdrew to crash again,
as they did when you were here beside her.

Salt water claimed the air,
wet sand the shore,
seagulls the sky.
She claimed this time—
the very thing you had so little of,
to spend with thoughts of you.

# Almost November

I wake this dark morning
to sounds of winds so strong,
trees bend in their directions,
leaves tear from their connections,
passion in the air.

Dense gray clouds—
rain pours down at an angle,
tires splash onto sidewalks,
drenched cat comes in to stay.

I expect to *batten down the hatches,*
keep mayhem outside
but when I open up the door
to my surprise, it's warm.

So I welcome into my home
for awhile these wet winds,
their sounds and smells—
the passion can stay.

# Candlelight

When the lights went out
I lit a candle.
Stormy clouds took over,
low ceiling of gloom.
Lightning struck,
for a second it was daylight.

Overgrown garden obscured
through glass, misty rain.

I wrote a letter on parchment paper
with a feather quill pen,
folded it in three, sealed it
with melted wax.
All my dreamy ideas
locked into written words on a page.

I'll reread it in years to come,
see if I feel the same.

# About the Author

Kathaleen Donnelly is a 1976 graduate of St. Vincent's Hospital School of Nursing, which was in Greenwich Village, NYC. She has lived on Long Island all her life, retired from Stony Brook University Hospital after 40 years, having spent the last 20 as a nurse practitioner in the Cardiology Department, now per diem. Her son Keith was born in 1977 and now lives in California with his wife Annie.

The Sweetbriar Nature Camera Club, part of the Photographic Federation of Long Island, helped Donnelly learn what makes a good photograph. She edited three anthologies: *Paumanok, Poems and Pictures of Long Island* (2009), *Paumanok, Interwoven* (2013), and *Paumanok, Transition* (2022).

She began writing poetry in her 50s. Her work has appeared or been pubhlished in the following publications: *Bards Annual, CEED: Center for Environmental Education and Discovery, Childhood, Gallery North, Long Island Newspaper, Long Island Quarterly, Long Island Sounds: An Anthology of Poetry from Maspeth to Montauk and Beyond, Nassau County Poet Laureate Review, Oberon, The Performance Poets Association Literary Review, Poems of Illness and Healing, The Seventh Quarry, Songs of Seasoned Women, Suffolk County Poetry Review, A Taste of Poetry, Towards Forgiveness, Whispers and Shouts,* and *Writing Outside the Lines.*

See her work at:
poetographyLongIsland.com

# Praise for *See If I Feel the Same*

*See If I Feel the Same* is a compelling collection of poems inspired by life experiences. As you meet the spirit of Kathaleen, she will take you on a memorable journey, turning calendar pages of seasons to share a different glimpse of the world. As a medical professional she will trigger your emotions. Yet, humorously, the poem Aging Remedy features the life clock as it turns backwards. Kathaleen has the ability to stir the conscious mind and an appetite to satisfy the spirit with her words. As you read through the pages of See if I Feel the Same you will be certain to find a space where you feel the same as you hear this peaceful poet roar.

—Robert Savino, Suffolk County Poet Laureate, New York (2015–2017)

Kathaleen Donnelly's poetry collection is a beautiful reflection of the author's unique life experiences and worldview. Through her words, she delves into primal subjects such as love, grief, fear, and hope while also expressing her admiration for the abundant beauty of our planet. Donnelly's skillful use of language and a keen eye for detail create a captivating word magic that builds poem after poem, crafting a refined and authentic voice that draws the reader in. With meditations from present and past memories, the author invites us to contemplate the dualities we face and how we reconcile ourselves to our world. If you are a poetry lover, this book is a must-have for your collection.

—Gladys L. Henderson, Suffolk County Poet Laureate, New York (2017–2019)

*See If I Feel the Same* is a book of daily reflections and observations, interspersed with poems of what it means to be a nurse, or how one attempts to live with the ever—present specter of war. You can accompany her to an I.C.U. unit in the hospital, where life is held in fragile balance, then join the poet on her spiritually renewing walks down Cordwood Path to the Sound ("Winter Walk"). This is the balance we are all searching for.

—Barbara Southard, Suffolk County Poet Laureate, New York (2019–2021)

www.ingramcontent.com/pod-product-compliance
Lightning Source LLC
Chambersburg PA
CBHW022016160426
43197CB00007B/456